Transformation
Marketing For Upscale Equine Facilities

THE SECRET TO BECOMING THE ONLY HORSE FACILITY IN YOUR MARKET

PATRICIA RESZETYLO

Transformation Marketing For Upscale Equine Facilities:
The Secret To Becoming The ONLY Horse Facility In Your Market

Copyright © 2014 by Patricia Reszetylo.

All rights reserved. Printed in the United States of America. No part of this book may be used or reproduced in any manner whatsoever without written permission except in the case of brief quotations embodied in critical articles or reviews.

For information contact the author at:
http://TransformationMarketingBook.com

ISBN: 1502583836

ISBN-13: 978-1502583833

First Edition: October, 2014

10 9 8 7 6 5 4 3 2 1

Table of Contents

ACKNOWLEDGEMENTS VIII

INTRODUCTION X

HOW TO USE THIS BOOK XIV

ABOUT THE AUTHOR XV

CHAPTER 1 SECRET ELIMINATES YOUR COMPETITION 1
    TRANSFORMATION 1A 1
    TRANSFORMATION 2B 2

CHAPTER 2 SECRET ESTABLISHES YOU AS AUTHORITY 3
    TRANSFORMATION 2 4

CHAPTER 3 SECRET: A SIMPLE SYSTEM FOR THIS YEAR 5
    TRANSFORMATION 3 6

CHAPTER 4 NO CHANGES IN YOUR LIFE? 7
    TRANSFORMATION 4: GOAL SETTING 9

CHAPTER 5 SECRET BREAKS THRU MARKETING CLUTTER 11
    TRANSFORMATION 5 13

CHAPTER 6 SECRET ESTABLISHES DEEP TRUST 15
    TRANSFORMATION 6 16

CHAPTER 7 SECRET: HOW TO FIRE 80% OF YOUR HERD 17
    TRANSFORMATION 7: 19

CHAPTER 8 SECRET THAT MULTIPLIES YOUR PROFITS 21
    TRANSFORMATION 8 22

CHAPTER 9 SECRET: NO HOPE MARKETING ALLOWED! 25
    TRANSFORMATION 9 27

CHAPTER 10 SECRET: UNDERSTANDING CLIENT VALUE 29

TRANSFORMATION 10: CUSTOMER VALUES 29

CHAPTER 11 SECRET: YOU CAN HAVE PERFECT MARKETING 35

CHAPTER 12 SECRET: HOW TO MAKE BEST USE OF YOUR MARKETING $$ 37

CHAPTER 13 39

SECRET: 18 MARKETING STRATEGIES FOR USING A BOOK TO MASSIVELY GROW YOUR HORSE FACILITY'S BUSINESS 39

STRATEGY #1 – LOCAL MEDIA 39
TRANSFORMATION: 41
STRATEGY #2 – NATIONAL MEDIA 42
TRANSFORMATION: 44
STRATEGY #3 – LOCAL, REGIONAL, & NATIONAL HORSE ASSOCIATIONS 45
TRANSFORMATION: 46
STRATEGY #4 – REGIONAL, NATIONAL, & ACTIVITY SPECIFIC MAGAZINES 47
TRANSFORMATION: 48
STRATEGY #5 – MAIL 49
TRANSFORMATION: 50
STRATEGY #6 – LEAD GENERATION BY MAIL 52
TRANSFORMATION: 52
STRATEGY #7 – INCENTIVIZE INITIAL APPOINTMENTS 53
TRANSFORMATION: 53
STRATEGY #8 – FOLLOW UP WITH UNCONVERTED PROSPECTS 54
TRANSFORMATION: 54
STRATEGY #9 – GIVE AS A "THANK YOU" GIFT 55
TRANSFORMATION: 55
STRATEGY #10 – CAPTURE LEADS ON WEBSITE 56
TRANSFORMATION: 58
STRATEGY #11 – SEND IT AS A GIFT 59
TRANSFORMATION: 60
STRATEGY #12 – BUILD A PROMOTION 61
TRANSFORMATION: 61
STRATEGY #13 – NETWORKING ON STEROIDS 62

TRANSFORMATION: 62
STRATEGY #14 – "MEET THE AUTHOR" 63
TRANSFORMATION: 63
STRATEGY #15 – CREATE A SEMINAR 64
TRANSFORMATION: 64
STRATEGY #16 – CREATE VIDEO OR AUDIO SEMINARS 65
TRANSFORMATION: 67
STRATEGY #17 – ONLINE MARKETING 68
TRANSFORMATION: 68
STRATEGY #18 – HOW TO USE YOUR BOOK TO GENERATE REFERRALS 70
TRANSFORMATION 13: REFERRALS STRATEGY 72

CHAPTER 14 FREQUENTLY ASKED QUESTIONS 75

DIRECT RESPONSE MARKETING VS. "HOPE" MARKETING 75
WHY DO "I" (OR MY BUSINESS) NEED A BOOK? 75
WHAT IS THE RIGHT WAY TO SET UP MY BOOK? 76
WHAT IS THE "RIGHT WAY" TO SET UP MY WEBSITE? 76
HOW CAN A BOOK "FENCE IN" MY HERD (CLIENTS)? 77
HOW DO I GET WORD OUT ABOUT MY NEW BOOK? 77
WHY SHOULD I LET YOU DO IT FOR ME INSTEAD OF A GHOSTWRITER I KNOW? 78
WHAT IS YOUR PROCESS? 80

NEXT STEP: 82

CONCLUSION 83

GLOSSARY 85

Acknowledgements

A book is a serious investment of time, energy, and emotion. It's the statement of the journey of a person, none of which can be accomplished totally by oneself. "No Man Is An Island," as they say. So the acknowledgements of a book are really the acknowledgement of what - of WHO -made the author, and who sent them on their journey

The last seven years of my life have been magnificent. I've gone to the deepest depths of my soul, and made it out the other side. Many people, as the news of famous actors dying from depression show, don't survive that journey.

I have my mother, **Juanita Goff**, and my sister, **Rebecca Wilkins**, to thank for sending me on that journey. Without you, I'd have floundered happily along, and never been forced to see who I really am.

My dear husband **John**, and our two special needs boys, who supported me and never stopped believing in me during all those dark days; who stayed by my side as I crunched through my marketing learning curve, and who I love totally.

My horses through the years, as they each brought me a step closer to who I am today. Especially close to my heart are **Rosey** and **Sparky**. I know I'll see you all again.

So many horse people through the years, starting with **Val Butterfield**, **Rosealee Mellor**, and others.

My marketing mentors, including **Ellen Violette**, my first coach, who got me up and running. **Joe Nicassio**, my next coach, who brought me into the world of direct response marketing, and really expanded my wings. **Dan Kennedy**, who's with me via his multitude of books and programs. Jay Abraham, who's there in similar fashion.

My customers down through the years, as well as all the lovely people I have been blessed to interview - and some that I did NOT interview!

Benny Valenzuela, for connecting with me and inviting me into his mastermind group on Facebook. I've gotten more out of that group than I'll ever be able to articulate. Thank you Benny, and thank you to so many of the members of that group for supporting me.

Roger Abramson, whom I met in Benny's group, and who has seen things in me I didn't know existed, and who is a wonderful mentor and coach.

And last but certainly NOT least, **Samanta**, who brings the world together and has given my life a whole new dimension.

Introduction
Dear Equine Facility Owner and/or Manager,

You are to be commended! Your facility is a class act! You've put many hours, and many dollars into creating a thing of beauty. Your horses and clients are happy with your facility and your services.

And yet, there's a cloud on the horizon, isn't there? There's always the threat that the stable down the road, or on the other side of the county will take your clients that you've worked SO hard to bring in.

YES, I'm suggesting we LITERALLY transform your business so transparently yet so decisively that your competition doesn't know what happened. All they know is that *you* now have all the best clients and horses, and they are left with the DUDs.

I'm not suggesting that we rent a backhoe or a bulldozer and literally plow all your completion into the ground.

But when we're done, you'll notice that you have so "fenced in" your own "herd" of clients, starting with your current ones, and then extending that to your well-indoctrinated prospects, that it's *as if* your competition doesn't exist, for all the effect they'll have on your business.

Because you *do* want to keep them in business. After all, you need somewhere to refer the clients you no longer want, or the ones that you simply can't take on.

Ok? Let's take this from the top.

You love horses. You always have. And to continue to enjoy them, you're required to market your stable, your training services, your riding instruction, and whatever else you do.

Perhaps you want to compete at high levels. For that you need sponsorship, if you aren't personally wealthy.

Or you need the client with the competition horse, but who isn't up to campaigning him herself. Or the wealthy client who sponsors you to campaign this horse for the client...

One of the quickest ways to reach your IDEAL Client (or sponsor – or both) is to do savvy marketing things your competition does NOT do – things that differentiate you from them, in a positive way.

If you do the things they do, how do your potential clients KNOW that they want to come to your stable? Copying others' marketing is just marketing incest.

It does NOT differentiate you from your competition, leaving you with the Small Fish/Big Pond Syndrome.

It's also the quickest way to the lowest common denominator, which in marketing is price. Marketing with price as your competitive advantage is the quickest way to run yourself out of business.

Good-bye IDEAL clients, hello DUDS.

Even the big stores, such as Wal-Mart™ who DO compete on price, only do so as a **perception**. They want you to THINK they are the low price leader. Here's a secret: even **they** are abandoning that approach.

They can see where the "low-price leader" path leads.

So can you. So you know you have to do something different.

You may already be working in that direction. That alone makes you an ideal candidate to learn this strategy.

This is by no means a NEW strategy. It is one that has been successfully used for hundreds, if not thousands, of years.

We're going to give your direct competitors "the boot" in the eyes of your clients and your potential clients.. giving YOUR business the *Leg Up* you desire.

Imagine building a competitor-proof "fence" around your herd of IDEAL clients. When you use what you'll learn in this little book, you can do just that. And even better, you can influence potential IDEAL clients that are still outside that fence, and draw them in.

~The Secret To Become The ONLY Horse Facility In Your Market ~

How to Use this Book

This book is meant to be used as a guidebook to direct you into a high impact-on-your-market strategy. For this strategy to work for you, we compile information which we then leverage, or in some cases, use as markers to show progress.

So find a quiet, comfortable, well-lit place to read – and write. Have a

- Cup of coffee or tea at hand.
- A highlighter - yes, mark this book up. It's YOURS! You learn better when you have stuff highlighted.
- A writing pen, so you can do the Transformation exercises in the book. And do them IN the book – it's all set up for you, and there are real psychological reasons to do the assignments in order – they build on each other.
- You may want to have your bookkeeping and a calculator close at hand. I'll ask you to do some number stuff in some of the Transformation exercises. Don't worry, it's pretty simple stuff.

You may find that it takes several sessions to get through this book, especially as you do the assignments, but you'll come out with a much better view of your business, your target market, what you want to achieve with both your business and your life – and the real capacity of your business!

> Don't Wait! Right now, before your competition learns about this, and while I can still offer these sessions, go *directly* to page 81 and apply to qualify for your $197 value assessment to start transforming *your* facility from Great to

About The Author

I'm Patricia Reszetylo, a life-long equestrian and business student. My best teachers have been a plethora of other business students, including Dr Richard Bandler, Dan S. Kennedy, and Jay Abraham, to name a few of the greats.

I've also ran a number of businesses - of which some were more successful than others, but all of which were learning laboratories, networking and launching boards for future enterprises.

I've been blessed with great horses, great friends, great customers, and great marketing minds to call upon.

I'm known in the horse industry for doing teleseminars, webinars, and Google Hangouts long before they were popular.

And now I'm handing YOU a business strategy so brilliant you'd think it was concieved just yesterday.. but it wasn't. In fact it's been around for a VERY long time...

Happy Trails!

Patricia Reszetylo,
October, 2014

Chapter

1

Secret Eliminates Your Competition

Competition is fierce these days. Even though the economy is coming back into its own, here in late 2014, due to the recent recession, consumers are still skeptical of the claims you make in the marketplace. They want to be sure when they spend money that it brings them real value.

No, they don't trust your claims. With more and more people who believe the government needs to hand out more and more aid; people who believe that "the middle class is shrinking," and that THAT is a BAD thing; even more incidents of those who are supposed to protect us violently accosting innocent bystanders, nobody trusts anybody these days.

<u>Wouldn't it be great if you could:</u>

- ☐ Essentially **"get rid of"** your competition?
- ☐ Have your pick of the **best clients and horses** in your market?
- ☐ *Not* worry that another, *inferior* stable or trainer can steal your best clients?
- ☐ Send your **DUD clients** to other stables?

Well, now you can.

<u>**In the little book which you now hold in your hands, I'll show you how to achieve ALL FOUR goals faster and easier than you might imagine.**</u>

Transformation 1A: Take a pen and check each box in the list above that IS something you'd <u>like</u> to achieve in the next 6-12 months.

TRANSFORMATION 2B: On the lines below, write **what achieving them means to you**:

1. _____

2. _____

3. _____

4. _____

This is a very important Transformation Item. Don't just skip ahead to the next chapter.

Chapter

2

Secret Establishes You As Authority

If you did the first 2 Transformations, congratulate yourself! You've just done more for yourself than most businesses EVER do to make life easy for themselves. **Award yourself a nice, big carrot!**

You didn't? Stop right now, go back to the Transformation, and do your homework! **No carrots for you until you do!**

We are swamped with advertising messages. Billboards, advertisements, and marketing statements are everywhere these days. There is NO escaping them. Now that we are connected with our devices, there are even more – and the net result is that we don't pay as much attention to not just the advertising messages, but to anything!

As a business person looking to make a statement in your market, you have to find ways to stand out from the clutter in order to get your message to your market *before* your competition gets their hooks into *your* Ideal Client.

What are the best things to do to achieve that? I find it's a process with 3 basic elements, a complete strategy to implement, rather than just using a tactic here or there:

- Know your **market**
- Craft your **message** to *that* market
- Deliver it via the best **medium** for *that* market.

The best strategies create an ongoing marketing funnel, if you will, that consistently attracts, qualifies, develops, and moves the client forward into your sales process.

Establishing yourself as the foremost authority in your market is an absolutely essential piece of the strategy. In fact, using the above strategy *automatically* sets you up as an authority in your market.

TRANSFORMATION 2: Answer the following questions:

a) What specific market do I want to dominate? Consider the following aspects: geographic, discipline, skill level, age, financials, etc.

_____

_____

_____

b) What message is most important to communicate to them?

_____

_____

This is a very important Transformation Item. Don't just skip ahead to the next chapter.

Chapter

3

Secret: A Simple System For This Year

If you did the first 3 Transformations, congratulate yourself! You've just done more for yourself than most businesses EVER do to make life easy for themselves. **Award yourself a nice, big carrot!**

You didn't? Stop right now, go back to the Transformation, and do your homework! **No carrots for you until you do!**

As an equestrian, you can easily spend the next 20-40 years training, teaching, competing, and giving clinics in order to set yourself up as an expert or as an authority... and while you might be the best equestrian on the planet, you could still die in obscurity.

Plenty of fabulous equestrians do.

OR you could write (the RIGHT book), market it (the RIGHT way), and establish yourself as an authority *THIS* year.

Why? Because when you're an author, especially of a book, people **automatically** respect you. You are given **opportunities** not extended to regular, mere mortals. People assume you are not only an expert, but THE BEST at what you do.

Only experts write books, right? And it takes years of blood, sweat and tears to write a book.. and pure genius to market it, right?

I'm going to let you in on some of the BEST kept secrets in marketing.

No, you don't have to be a world-renown expert to write a book.

No, It doesn't take forever to write a GOOD one, and if it's done right, it doesn't take a river of blood, sweat and tears.

Marketing isn't rocket science. It only takes an understanding of who you are trying to reach, what issues they have – and which of those you are able to solve well. It does, take a technical understanding of what is available to use, what technology can and cannot do, and how people respond to marketing messages.

When your book is written (and marketed) correctly, it turns into one of the BEST lead-generation tools available to modern equestrians.

Yes, there are a few tricks to it.

And I'll help you connect better with your market than you ever DREAMED possible – I have more than a few tricks up my sleeve, along with connections you don't!

TRANSFORMATION 3: 5 Reasons I Want To Be An Authority Figure In My Market:

Grab your pen, and start writing! Yes, make a list **right here**:

1. _____

2. _____

3. _____

4. _____

5. _____

This is a very important Transformation Item. Don't just skip ahead to the next chapter.

Chapter

4

No Changes In Your Life?

If you did the first 4 Transformations, congratulate yourself! You've just done more for yourself than most businesses EVER do to make life easy for themselves. **Award yourself a nice, big carrot!**

You didn't? Stop right now, go back to the Transformations, and do your homework! **No carrots for you until you do!**

Our business goals often come from our personal goals.. which then take a back seat to the business goal. Now we have clients that need lessons, horses trained and cared for, competed, promoted.. and we forget why we went into business in the first place.

Why did YOU go into business in the horse industry? Was it so you could work 12-18 hour days? Was it so you could be tied to the barn and your clients, with no life of your own?

As equestrians, we usually go into business in the industry because we love horses. We enjoy riding. We enjoy training. We enjoy instructing other equestrians.

We start CHARGING for those services for 2 reasons:

- The client has more respect for the work we do when **they** pay,
- We, like everybody else, have bills to pay.

How much we charge is based on how much **we** feel we deserve for the activity. If we're insecure, or we don't know how to sell our services, we often charge "only what others are charging." We compete on price. We sell ourselves out.

We're told that "working hard to get what we want" is called "having a work ethic," and that it's a good thing.

It can be. When we work hard, practice what we do best, we get very good at what we do. And THAT is a good thing!

But it can be a BAD thing to put off any kind of attainable rewards for that elusive, traditionally acquired carrot of "When you finally are 'established.'"

Why do we have to accept that the standard, traditionally accepted path to authority status is the ONLY path.. <u>especially</u> when there are other paths available?

Let me explain.

Yes, you do need to do GOOD work (The rest is just marketing).

There are people in this world who REALLY stand out. They aren't any better than you are. They didn't have any advantages that you didn't. Why did they get ahead so easily.. and you're still struggling?

It's likely they took ADVANTAGE of an opportunity that you did not. That is a very easy thing to fix – and that's the purpose of this book – to show you how to take advantage of some secrets that you may have not known were available to you.

Let's get back to our original goals.

We know that setting goals is one of the first things we need to do to achieve them. What are your goals in life? What do you want to achieve for yourself, your business, your family, your clients?

What dreams did you have as a child? How many of those have you achieved? What is in your "bucket list?"

TRANSFORMATION 4: GOAL SETTING

Grab your pen, and start writing! Yes, make a list **right here**:

1. _____

2. _____

3. _____

4. _____

5. _____

6. _____

7. _____

8. _____

9. _____

10. _____

This is a very important Transformation Item. Don't just skip ahead to the next chapter.

Chapter

5

Secret Breaks Thru Marketing Clutter

If you did the first 5 Transformations, congratulate yourself! You've just done lots more for your business than most businesses EVER do to make life easy for themselves. **Award yourself a nice, big carrot!**

You didn't? Stop right now, go back to the Transformation, and do your homework! **No carrots for you until you do!**

How many marketing message do you encounter on a daily basis? Between radio, TV, internet, email, billboards, signage, flyers, advertisements, and a thousand other marketing mediums, you encounter enough to overwhelm a stadium full of people. So your brain does what it does best: instead of shutting down, it organizes information via filters.

- "This is important. We'll remember this."
- "This is an ad. We won't pay any attention to it."

Some estimate that we are exposed to 30,000 or more marketing messages EVERY day!

How's that for clutter!?

In order to break through that mess, to reach your IDEAL client, you need to do something radically different. Something special. Something that positions you as an authority. Something that gets you paid for WHO you are, rather than for WHAT you are.

A book is special, as we mentioned, because people now treat *you* differently. **You are a *published author*,** after all! *They* could never write a book (as if only special people can write books)!

And the media likes to talk about new books too. It's much, *much* easier to get interviews on T.V., radio or with a newspaper when they have a book to talk about than if you were going to get one to talk about you, your business, your stable.

So, first we write an amazing book that your best customer finds extremely useful. Then we share it with your local media. They don't know about it until we tell them in a unique and creative fashion.

Even before the media asks you for an interview, we set it up so they ask you for background info. How is it that you are this amazing expert that could write this book? That's when you talk about you, your history, your stable, your stallion... whatever it is that you are really trying to market.

So a book is an easy way to get into those interviews in the first place – and then there are wonderful ways to leverage any media exposure so that you can extend the effect.

When dealing with the general public, at least the general public in your target market, you'll find that your book, and the resulting media, turns you into a hero, an icon, somebody that people are amazed will talk to them. You'll have people come up to you and ask things like, "Are you that author?" When you affirm you are, they will squeal and laugh and ask for your autograph. YOU haven't changed – their perception of you has changed, and that's what we want.

You think you're just sweaty from cleaning stalls. They say, "She's so down to earth…"

If you've never had a media interview before, don't worry. There are easy ways to make it easy for both YOU and the interviewer.

Now, take 5 minutes to write out 5 questions you DO want to answer in a media interview. You can also write down 5 sub topics that we can develop questions around.

TRANSFORMATION 5: Questions I *WANT* to Media To Ask Me:

Yes, take 5-10 minutes to make a list here:

1. _____
2. _____
3. _____
4. _____
5. _____

Chapter

6

Secret Establishes Deep Trust

If you did the first 6 Transformations, congratulate yourself! You've just done lots more for yourself than most businesses EVER do to make life easy for themselves. **Award yourself a nice, big carrot!**

You didn't? Stop right now, go back to the Transformation, and do your homework! **No carrots for you until you do!**

We've just been through the deepest recession since the 70's. Many of your clients may not have even been born then, or if they were around, they don't remember it, as they were just too young to be aware.

I promise you this: They won't forget this one anytime soon.

Millions of people out of work, coupled with millions of overpriced, over-leveraged homes repossessed, made for a scary 5 or 6 years. Many stables and breeding operations went under, sending their horses to rescues or to slaughter.

People stopped going to shows, stopped training, and stopped taking riding lessons. Everything came to a screeching halt for many. The middle class had money.. but was NOT spending it.

It was a confidence issue, not an availability issue. Things are picking up as I write this in mid-2014, but for those who've been through this, *they'll never forget it.*

Every purchase has to count. Everything must HAVE measurable value, as compared to pre-recessionary days, where people bought stuff just because it was there.

And even more than that, they have to trust YOU.

Publishing a book has an interesting side effect: it increases your personal perceived value. Now that you have a published book to your name, your interaction with them has more value:

- **You're an established authority**, even more than you were before. What you say and do *means* more, is more important and more valuable.
- **You have "star power."** For example, any pretty girl can sex up a car. But put a celebrity in that same car, and it multiplies the sexiness of it. That is why the star's name is so valuable. The same holds true in your business.
- **You'll attract more of your "best qualified" IDEAL clients** to your business, which means you can let go of your "less qualified" clients. Now you're getting paid better, and doing more of what you love, less of what you don't. Your time is more valuable now!
- **You've established solid reasons for them to trust you** – "After all, she wrote a book on it, she knows what she's talking about."

TRANSFORMATION 6: 4 Ways My Authority Benefits My Clients:

Yes, take 5-10 minutes to make a list here:

1. _____
2. _____
3. _____
4. _____

Chapter

7

Secret: How To Fire 80% of Your Herd

If you did the first 7 Transformations, congratulate yourself! You've just done lots more for yourself than most businesses EVER do to make life easy for themselves. **Award yourself a nice, big carrot!**

You didn't? Stop right now, go back to the Transformation, and do your homework! **No carrots for you until you do!**

Ever heard of the Pareto Principle? Management consultant Joseph M. Juran suggested the principle and named it after Italian economist Vilfredo Pareto, who observed in 1906 that 80% of the land in Italy was owned by 20% of the population.

It is a common rule of thumb in business; e.g., "80% of your sales come from 20% of your clients". Mathematically, the 80-20 rule is roughly followed by a power law distribution (also known as a Pareto distribution) for a particular set of parameters, and many natural phenomena have been shown empirically to exhibit such a distribution.

Writing a book and marketing it the way we do is direct response marketing. Any marketing that does not rely on "brand awareness" or "getting the message in front of prospects many times" might be direct response marketing (DRM). The magic comes from understanding the market you are targeting, learning what makes them tick, what your solution does for them, then using that knowledge along with skilled writing to capture their attention, and get them to act NOW.

Mesmerizing them with pink, clapping bunnies[i1] to sell your batteries isn't DRM. Capturing their attention with a great headline, getting your message

---

[1] Which brand of batteries does the bunny sell? **See endnote i**

to resonate with them, and then giving them a great reason to act NOW *is* DRM.

As a small business, you have different values and objectives than a huge national corporation does. They have egos to stroke, and investors to keep happy. You need to focus on keeping your clients happy – and in getting new ones with the most efficiency possible.

When I work with a client to write a book to assist them in marketing their equine operation, I always start out with a pile of questions:

- What problem(s) do you solve? What does your best customer look like?
- Who are your competitors?

How do you know who is your best customer? Who spends the most money with you, and at the same time, is the least hassle? With whom do you have the best profit margin? Who do you want more of?

We can look at this from the opposite end too: Who is your DUD customer? Who costs you the most in time and/or money (as time IS money)? Who pays you the least, nitpicks over stuff, gripes over paying (or maybe pays late); insists on cafeteria-style rather than package-based buying? Who gives you the most headaches, and is the biggest pain in the ass?

The Pareto Principle says that 80% of your profits come from 20% of your herd. That means that you can cull much of the *80%*, if you replace them with more clients like the *20%*. Knowing WHO they are is the first step. So I ask, "Which ones would YOU cull, if you could?"

TRANSFORMATION 7: Who's My Best Customer?

7.A.: Names of my best customers over the years (don't worry, this is your book, nobody else will see it):

Yes, make a list here:

1. _____
2. _____
3. _____
4. _____

Transformation 7.B.: So let's look again at those BEST customers again.

What characteristics do they all have in common? Yes, make a list here:

1. _____
2. _____
3. _____
4. _____
5. _____

Transformation 7.C: What Problem(s) Do I Solve For My Customer?

Take 5-10 minutes to write down problem(s) you solve for your **best** customers:

Yes, make a list here:

1. _____
2. _____
3. _____

4. _____

5. _____

Transformation 7.d Which Clients Would I CULL (If I could)?

You don't need to name names. Just write down the characteristics of your DUD clients:

1. _____

2. _____

3. _____

4. _____

5. _____

These are very important Transformation Items. Take 10 minutes and do it - don't just skip ahead to the next chapter.

CHAPTER

8

SECRET THAT MULTIPLIES YOUR PROFITS

If you did the first 10 Transformations, congratulate yourself! You've just done lots more for yourself than most businesses EVER do to make life easy for themselves. **Award yourself a nice, big carrot!**

You didn't? Stop right now, go back to the Transformation, and do your homework! **No carrots for you until you do!**

Let's go back to why you need a book, how it should be set up to operate as a direct marketing tool, how to leverage the website so they all work as a powerful marketing strategy.. not just as separate tactics.

First, we use the book to set up a conversation with your BEST potential customer. But we don't set up just **any** conversation - we set up the conversation **WE want them to have**.

We'll use the book to educate them - and even beyond that, to **indoctrinate them** - to your way of thinking, operating, and working. Now you have people a group of people who:

- **Understand and like your process** of riding, training, and/or caring for their horse;
- Can decide if they LIKE it and want to work with you, **or** dislike it, and therefore **won't hassle you** with months of slow death before they finally pack up and leave;
- Are literally *inoculated* **mentally** against going to other stables, trainers or instructors,
- And **are willing to jump through hoops** to get in to work with you.

Your website is one of the hoops they have to jump through in order to work with you. They HAVE to approach you in a specific manner, or they are not qualified to board their horse, take lessons, get their horse trained, or even to ask you to campaign their horse – whatever it is you do.

Why should we make them jump through hoops to get to you? Why don't we make it easy to get in?

BECAUSE: We want to **disqualify as many as possible**, so you can focus on working with the few who **do** fit your IDEAL Client Profile.

TRANSFORMATION 8

Looking at your revenue-producing activities, make a list of the ones that you enjoy the most, starting with your favorite, and ending with the least enjoyable.

1. _____

2. _____

3. _____

4. _____

Now order your revenue-producing activities starting with the MOST profitable, and ending with the least.

1. _____

2. _____

3. _____

4. _____

c: Go back and make a tick mark beside each that is on BOTH lists. This is a very important Transformation Item.

Here is another way to look at the last 3 Transformations:

The overlap between your (1) Competency Area Activities and (2) the MOST profitable activities are (3) where you need to spend most of your time and energy. You'll enjoy the work more, you'll make more money, and your clients will be happier, more likely to stay longer, pay more, and refer more clients like themselves into the business.

Note that your IDEAL clients (the 20% that bring in the 80% of the profits) usually fall into this overlap area.

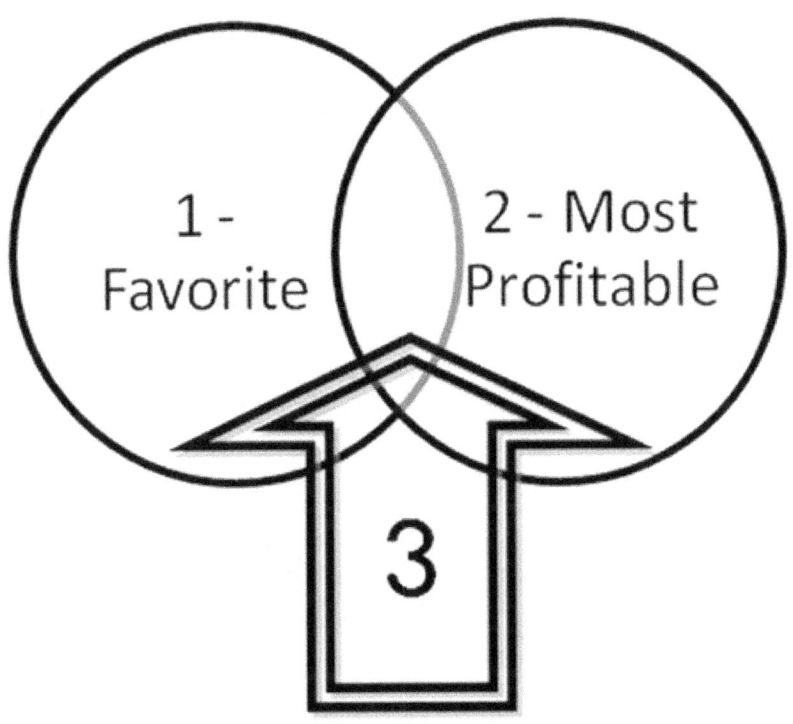

Doing this transformation sets you up for this cycle:

1. You enjoy your work MORE, which allows you to give your herd BETTER service... which leads to more enjoyment for both you AND your herd.
2. Better service and happier clients leads to more profits, and more referrals, which leads back to happier clients and more enjoyment, in turn leading to a continuous upward cycle.

CHAPTER

9

SECRET: NO HOPE MARKETING ALLOWED!

If you did the first 12 Transformations, congratulate yourself! You've just done lots more for yourself than most businesses EVER do to make life easy for themselves. **Award yourself a nice, big carrot!**

You didn't? Stop right now, go back to the Transformation, and do your homework! **No carrots for you until you do!**

What is "Hope Marketing"?

Hope Marketing is:

- when you think that all you have to do is "**hang out your shingle**" and that people will just come and buy your stuff.
- pretending you're a BIG BRAND, and that big-company **BRANDING-type marketing will make sales**.
- when you HOPE your marketing is working, even though you aren't tracking it, and **you don't know how people find you**. If they find you at all.
- And worst of all, "Hope Marketing" has been popularized by T.V. and movies. You see so many movies where people put extraordinary effort into things, but the bad guy still repossesses the shop because the owner merely HOPED that her extra special muffins or cookies would do the trick on their own.

The polar opposite of "Hope Marketing" is Direct Response Marketing. This is marketing that:

- **KNOWS what the target market is looking for – AND – what words will spur them to Transformation NOW.**

- Doesn't concern itself with branding. BRANDING is a happy side effect of good marketing.
- **Tracks where people come from**, what marketing brought them in, as well as many other stats. Its marketing held accountable for production. If it doesn't *work*, it's *fired*.

Unless you have the need to randomly spend money on helping your ad agency win creative awards, or the need to stroke the egos of stockholders, you need to use Direct Response Marketing (DRM).

Still with me?

Great! Let's carry on!

While there are many strategies and tactics in DRM, it's best to start with looking at what you are currently doing, and finding ways to add tracking capabilities to it.

Here are some ways to do that:

- Add a "*dept #*" or "*dept. name*" to marketing that uses a mailing address, or which asks the person to make a phone call.
- *Keeping count on a list of your advertising places*, which you tick when a new client calls you, is useful.
- It may also work to *change the offer* you have them ask for, so that the different offers are indicative of where the advert was located.
- *Upgrade your website*. Switching from a "brochure-type" layout to one that forces an opt in to your email list, sometimes using an "ethical bribe," is widely used. Now you can also automate follow-up with an email sequence on an auto responder, as well as personally with emails or phone calls, as appropriate.
- Using a website in this manner allows you to send people coming from different sources, for example, from your book, or from your social media, to land on different pages. When they optin to your email list, that page is recorded, and you can track who came from

where – so now you know what marketing is working, and more importantly, *which marketing is NOT working!*

TRANSFORMATION 9: List your current advertising and marketing tactics – for example, "flyer at tackshop," "flyer at feed store." Then note if/how you are tracking each.

Yes, make a list here:

1. _____
   _____

2. _____
   _____

3. _____
   _____

4. _____
   _____

5. _____
   _____

This is a very important Transformation Item. Don't just skip ahead to the next chapter.

Chapter

10

Secret: Understanding Client Value

If you did the first 13 Transformations, congratulate yourself! You've just done lots more for yourself than most businesses EVER do to make life easy for themselves. **Award yourself a nice, big carrot!**

You didn't? Stop right now, go back to the Transformation, and do your homework! **No carrots for you until you do!**

On the flip side is the less enjoyable, less profitable customer.. and less enjoyable, less profitable activities. When you have all the IDEAL customers you can serve, you can let these less profitable ones go... freeing up resources so you can better serve your IDEAL customer, making you more profitable, so you can let more of the less profitable ones go... until you reach a happy balance point.

Why do you have DUD customers?

Because you don't know how to get (and keep) the IDEAL ones.

Transformation 10: Customer Values

First we look at the value of different segments of your customers. Most businesses don't have any idea how much value (profit) their customer brings to their business.

So first we look at AVERAGE customer value. Then we'll look at your IDEAL customers and then at your DUD customers.

Average Customer Value

Then segment your clients into BEST and DUD clients, and do it again. What are your:

- Average Customer Value (/yr):_____
- Average Lifetime Customer Value:_____
- IDEAL Client Value:_____
- IDEAL Client Lifetime Value:_____
- DUD Client Value:_____
- DUD CLV:_____

10.A.: Average Client Value: This takes your yearly profit, and divides it by the full number of clients you serviced(yes, write right in the book):

10.B: IDEAL Client Value: Now look at only your ideal clients, which may take a bit more work. Figure up your yearly profits from THEM, and divide by the number of IDEAL clients.

10.C: DUD Client Value: This is calculated from those on your "DUD" list. . Looking at ONLY your DUD clients, figure up your yearly profits, and divide by the number of DUD clients.

<u>Lifetime Client Value</u> – This is a VERY important Transformation Item, one that absolutely should not be skipped or skimped on.

<u>Life time</u>: How long does your client work with you? While there are some industry averages, you really have to look at your own numbers. This is a BENCHMARK number, one by which you will judge your progress. It may also be a defining value for your IDEAL and DUD clients, so it REALLY behooves you to look at your clients over the lifetime of your business, and figure out how long each stayed with you.

Note: Lifetimes may be measured in weeks, months or years. You'll have to see what your lowest measurement is. I have assumed "years" for the calculation, but yours may be measured in weeks or months.

<u>$/yr</u> : How much profit do they bring to your business yearly (or other time increment)?

10.D: <u>AVERAGE Client Lifetime Value:</u>

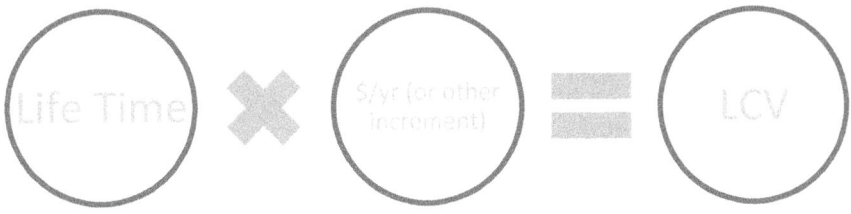

10.E: IDEAL Client Lifetime Value

10.F: DUD Client Lifetime Value

What do these numbers tell you? Here are some things they might tell you:

- How much you can spend to GET each into your operation;
- How much you can spend to KEEP each in your operation;
- Which you want MORE of, Which you want FEWER of.

When you can OUTSPEND your competition to GET and KEEP clients, you'll attract and keep better clients – but you *HAVE* to know how valuable they are to begin with!!

10.G: Personal Hourly Value This is an important number to track. The more you outsource lower-value work, the more you raise your personal hourly value, because now you focus on the more profitable, revenue-producing work.

What does this number tell you?

- What work you SHOULD do – and which you should outsource. Work that has less value than your hourly rate can be outsourced. You should be doing work that has higher per hour value.
- It gives you a starting point for determining your day rate.
- It gives you a point of reference to let you know if your operation is more or *less* profitable for you PERSONALLY.
- As you ADD more IDEAL clients, and CULL the DUDs, it goes up.

Whew! Did you make it through all that?

Yes, it's a LOT of work – but these numbers are critical to your business. And these are not numbers your accountant will ever generate for you – unless you specifically direct him to (and he'll probably grumble about it, too).

When you know your numbers, you know what you can or cannot spend on marketing, regardless of whether that is client acquisition or herd retention.

When you know your numbers, you know if you are working for less than minimum... or if you are actually creating wealth.

When you know what your numbers mean, you can better define IDEAL clients, cull the DUDs, freeing up resources for the IDEAL clients.. and for yourself.

Chapter

11

Secret: You Can Have Perfect Marketing

If you did the first 20 Transformations, congratulate yourself! You've just done lots more for yourself than most businesses EVER do to make life easy for themselves. **Award yourself a nice, big carrot!**

You didn't? Stop right now, go back to the Transformation, and do your homework! **No carrots for you until you do!**

It is possible to copy a book, and, with some work, even a complete website. While the odds of it happening are extremely slim, it's not unheard of.

Sending a **Digital Millennium Copyright Act**[2] (DMCA) take-down notification to the web hosting provider removes a copied website.

Yes, they'll be upset – but then they DIDN'T take advantage of my exclusive offer and guarantee to you.

Getting a copied book removed is a little more complicated. If a knocked-off book appears in your market, grab a copy of it and send it along to me. I'll help you verify that it's really and truly a knock off. If it is, that is also a copyright infringement issue, and may involve your attorney.

"Me-Too Marketing" – what we call it when somebody copies us – misses more than a few of the under-the-cover pieces we put into place, and is therefore much, much less effective.

---

[2] Digital Millennium Copyright Act, see more at http://en.wikipedia.org/wiki/Digital_Millennium_Copyright_Act

The big picture is that we are using a full-blown strategy, not just a few scattered tactics, to complement current marketing, and to build your full-blown marketing strategy. So many things go into crafting our strategy that it isn't something that can just be "knocked off."

Just like an iceberg that shows only 10% of its mass above the waterline, so your marketing only "shows" about 10% of what is going on.

Even if a competitor actually knows what is going on behind the scenes, they can't copy it – it would be individual and customized to them, not copied from you. So ironically, if they copy you, they do their own drilling down into their IDEAL client, they end up creating their own business-specific marketing, and in so doing, don't and can't directly copy you.

PLUS – I give you 18 strategies later on in this book that you can use with in conjunction with your own book to exponentially leverage your investment, and to multiply your presence, authority and celebrity status in your community – and especially in regards to your target market.

Some of these are things that you will personally do. Some of them are things that are best left to a professional. Some of them are so much work and so complicated, that most people simply throw their hands up in despair and won't do them.

But as you know, the difference between somebody who's a huge success, and one who isn't, is often the sheer volume or the degree of detail of what they are willing to do. Complicated is good. It works for us.

In a nutshell: your marketing won't be knocked off.

Chapter

12

Secret: How To Make Best Use Of Your Marketing $$

If you've done the Transformations in the previous chapters, you've laid the groundwork for a deeper marketing strategy. You've also done a lot more work than most businesses, large OR small, EVER do to understand their market and to hone their activities to bring in better customers.

Here are some ways to make the best use of your marketing resources:

1. <u>Make *all* marketing accountable</u>. Know where all segments of clients come from. If marketing doesn't pull, kill it. If you can't find SOME way of tracking it, don't use it. Advertising salespeople have (1) motive – to sell more advertising. They don't REALLY care, much less even know, if it's truly effective for you. Remember that – especially when they say things like "you need repetition" or that a client needs to hear your message X-# of times before they act. If your IDEAL client hears/sees your well-crafted message, they will respond. NOW.
2. <u>KNOW who you are trying to reach</u>. Build a profile of your IDEAL client. Build disqualifiers into your marketing, so unfit candidates disqualify themselves.
3. <u>Focus on the activities that are BOTH most personally enjoyable for you, AND which are most profitable</u>. Pick clients who use those, and cull those who don't. You'll enjoy your work more, you'll make more money, adding to the enjoyment; your clients, who are now getting better service, are happier, will stay with you longer and will spend more.
4. <u>Establish yourself as an authority and as a celebrity</u>. The best, and by far the easiest way to do this is to write the right book – and hook it into an appropriately-designed website. Juice those up with powerful

marketing. This sets up an amazing marketing machine, pumping IDEAL clients into your business, and streamlining profits.

5. **Start NOW.** Do the Transformation exercises. Look for ways to make your current marketing accountable. Your competition may be complacent today, but tomorrow they may decide to take action. Beat them to the punch – take action today.

Chapter 13

Secret: 18 Marketing Strategies For Using A Book To Massively Grow Your Horse Facility's Business

Strategy #1 - Local Media

The first strategy is to send media releases to your local and regional media outlets, including newspaper, radio stations, magazines, and T.V. Stations. A press release (or media release, as most like to call them) is an official communication to a media outlet to inform them of something specific. The GOAL of the media release is to do one or more of the following:

- *Get the media release published.*
- *Get somebody from that media to interview you*, write a story, which is then published to their readers, viewers or listeners.
- And/or *get the opportunity to be a contributor* to their media outlet.

In some cases, your media release might get published as-is, so you always want to end it with an invitation for readers to get a copy of your book – AND you always want to extend that invitation if you are actually interviewed too.

If you are invited to come on board as a contributor, you can use your book as content to publish in your column or a newsletter, so you don't even have to do any actual writing. *The BIG benefit here is you have the added credibility of using "John Doe, Author, and Contributor to (name of newspaper/TV station/Radio station/magazine)."*

Intimidated by getting on radio or tv? I can relate. Start even smaller. Host a coffee, where you autograph your book, and talk with locals. Do small talks for local groups. These will graduate into "bigger" presentations, and soon you'll be ready for radio and tv.

Why is media so important? Why do you NEED to get on radio and TV? Because we are changing the REASON people pay you. You currently get paid because you are GOOD (and no, that won't change, you'll still be good). But do you think that Kim Kardashian gets paid what she does because she's THAT good?

Not a chance. She gets paid what she does because she's a celebrity. Let her get old, fat, ugly - and off the air for a few years - and she's not worth much at all in Hollywood.

We are turning YOU into a celebrity. More people will want to work with you because you are a celebrity than because you're good.

Here's the secret formula:

(Good You)+(Celebrity) = much better paid YOU.

It also opens up doors, opportunities that would have otherwise passed you by. You'll be able to pick and choose your IDEAL clients, get rid of your DUD clients, and make more money and have more fun in the process.

NOW you're ready.

Transformation:

Make a list of all the local radio stations, TV stations, newspapers, and regional horse magazines in your area.

1. _____
2. _____
3. _____
4. _____
5. _____
6. _____
7. _____
8. _____
9. _____
10. _____
11. _____
12. _____
13. _____
14. _____
15. _____

Strategy #2 - National Media

You can use your book to get on national media such as ABC, NBC, CNN, FOX, Wall Street Journal, and others. As you are an equestrian[3], that includes the national/international horse-related magazines.

Once we've gotten you on local media, we leverage that into national media. Why don't we go national first?

- You need to hone your presentation (how you look) as well as what you say (how you say it).
- Each local media exposure is leveraged into a "sizzle reel" that we can use to help pitch you to the national guys.
- Your message may be local in nature, not national.

Once you've gotten on those national media, you'll add something that says "Author, As Seen on (whichever outlet)" to your business card, your website, your brochures – all of your marketing collateral – if you haven't done so with your local exposures.

AND of course, once you do that, you share it on all your social media profiles, websites, email newsletters, and any other place you communicate with your target market.

Think for just a moment about how using just these 2 marketing strategies will differentiate you from your competition. What did we just do?

We:

1. *Created a marketing piece* (the book) that we then leveraged first
2. LOCALLY. Media LOVES books, and especially loves local authors, so it's a safe bet it gets picked up locally and regionally;

---

[3] "Equestrian in the broad sense of the term, meaning somebody who works with horses, rather than just meaning "one who rides a horse".

3. *Then we took it national.* How many of your local competitors can say they've been on ABC or CNBC or CNN? That's right – not many of them.
4. Then we *got copies of those publications or broadcasts*, and we leveraged *that*, by making sure that both current clients and prospective ones, can read, see or hear this broadcast. AND there are other tricks one can do to leverage a tv appearance, which I share with my clients:

    For example: have a small crew do a "behind the scenes" shoot of you ON the set, and you share that everywhere and at every opportunity too.

Do you see how powerful this all is? If your target market knows about you, and your celebrity and authority status, that gives you a definitive edge over your competitors.

Let's look at this from the perspective of your potential client. If you are in the market looking for somebody to instruct you, to train your horse, to show your horse – whatever it is you do – would you go with somebody who's an author and has been on all these media platforms – a celebrity - or would you go with a nobody that hasn't?

Most people go with the celebrity. They're happy to pay more, too, and they have greater reason to refer other clients in – referrals are better clients all around anyway (they pay more, are less likely to leave, and are more likely to refer others too).

TRANSFORMATION:

What area do your clients come from – are they local, regional or national?

_____

What Nationally-based horse magazines address your specialty?

1. _____

2. _____

3. _____

4. _____

5. _____

6. _____

7. _____

8. _____

Strategy #3 – Local, Regional, & National Horse Associations

As horse business people and aficionados, we all belong to any number of horse-related associations. So do your target market – your IDEAL clients. Wouldn't it be amazing if those associations were to assist you in actually marketing your business?

I mean, beyond the member listing they so graciously give you as a paid member. And I also mean beyond the paid listings, or the sponsorship-granted marketing opportunities. What if you could do something so awesome that they would actually talk about you?

Writing your book is your first step. Getting it mentioned in local and regional media is the next step. Now you're going to send a few copies of your book, along with your very targeted media release, written specifically for each association, and copies of your locally and regionally garnered press.

Here's what you're looking for here:

- Perhaps they *just publish the press release*, which like all the others, invites the reader to your site for more info.
- Perhaps a bespoke *write up of the book*.
- *An interview* which they write up, or publish the audio or video of on their website.
- And again, perhaps the opportunity to contribute to their publications.

Again, this can be as targeted as you like – do you know how many thousands of horse associations, societies, clubs and whatnot there are in the United States alone? Thousands.

This just got interesting, didn't it?

TRANSFORMATION:

Local Horse Associations/Groups/Societies, etc that would benefit from hearing you give a talk:

1. _____
2. _____
3. _____
4. _____
5. _____

Regional/State-based Horse Associations/Groups/Societies, etc that would benefit from hearing you give a talk:

1. _____
2. _____
3. _____
4. _____
5. _____

National Horse Associations/Groups/Societies, etc that would benefit from hearing you give a talk:

1. _____
2. _____
3. _____
4. _____

Strategy #4 - Regional, National, & Activity Specific Magazines

How many horse publications are you aware of? While there are hundreds of nationally/internationally distributed magazines, there are nearly as many regional ones. And they are all looking for material to publish.

Some of these magazines are more targeted to your IDEAL client than others, so you MAY want to make a list of which ones to send to, depending on your:

- Location
- Geographic scope - are you a local, regional or nationally based company?
- Specialty - if you teach dressage, you want to target riders looking for dressage instruction, for example. While there are a few barrel racers who understand that dressage helps them ride better, most won't. Conversely, if you teach barrel racing, very few dressage riders will ever be interested.

So you'll send your packet of your book, your release, your interview questions, and any other materials you may have to your list of regional and national magazines.

Again, you're looking for them to:

- Get the media release published.
- Get somebody from that media to interview you, write a story, which is then published to their readers, viewers or listeners.
- And/or get the opportunity to be a contributor to their media outlet.

Now this really differentiates you from your competitors, doesn't it?

TRANSFORMATION:

National, Regional Horse Magazines that are relevant to you:

1. _____
2. _____
3. _____
4. _____
5. _____
6. _____
7. _____
8. _____
9. _____
10. _____
11. _____
12. _____
13. _____
14. _____
15. _____

Strategy #5 - Mail

Your business has geographic constraints. Your clients, IDEAL or otherwise will only drive so far in order to get to you. There is a limit, isn't there? If you hold clinics, that limit may be extended out to several hours - but they only come on an infrequent basis.

For regular instruction, people typically come from within a 30-45 minute drive.

So for a marketing strategy to reach those people, it's more efficient for them to come to you.

But here's how we can go to THEM.

We can mail your book to every address in a specific radius of your facility. As horse people are usually only a fraction of the population, that's still rather inefficient, so we can do the following two steps:

1. *We look at your IDEAL client's demographics*, pulling out characteristics that we can use to narrow down the list - rather than simply mailing to everybody in that specific radius, we're now mailing to affluent communities, people who've registered specific kinds of vehicles, etc.
2. *We can then take that list, and mail a copy of the book to each*, inviting them to visit your website, book an appointment, or to call a free recorded message - whatever action we decide we'd like them to take.

So is it useful to set geographic parameters or focus for your facility? Is it useful to target people of certain demographics, such as age, income, business owner or employee, homeowner or renter, owner of specific vehicles - such as a horse trailer?

If so, we can use this book mailing method to get in front of them.

Before you dismiss the idea of a mailing or say "Mail doesn't work," it's important to remember that when it comes to advertising or marketing, the success or failure of the effort to increase your sales is NOT THE RESULT of the media that you use.

If you tried social media, for example, and it didn't work, it isn't the fault of the social media site that you used.

If you tried an advertisement, or a flyer, and it didn't work, it isn't the advertisement or the flyer's fault. If you tried direct mail, and it didn't work, it isn't the fault of the post office, the mailman, or the mailing piece.

The problem lies with WHO you are attempting to sell to – and the MESSAGE you got in front of them.

When most business people think about increasing sales, the first thing they think is "Let's put an advert in the paper."

This is 100%, completely and totally, utterly wrong. You are literally putting the cart before the horse (although I've seen a picture where that worked).

The VERY first thing you MUST do is figure out EXACTLY *who* you want to talk to, and then *what* you'll say to them.

For example: think of a $1 bill and a $100 bill. Isn't the difference in value the message that's on the paper – NOT the paper itself? When advertising efforts don't work, it's usually not the fault of the ad. It's typically a problem with matching your message to your market.

Transformation:

My IDEAL client's characteristics:

Location: _____

Financial: _____

Age: _____

Other:

_____

_____

_____

Local areas of concentration of horse people (if known):

_____

_____

_____

Strategy #6 - Lead Generation By Mail

Another option with using Direct Mail, instead of simply mailing your book to even a targeted list in a given market area, is to mail out a postcard or letter inviting people to call your office (or visit your website, or call a free recorded message) and request a copy of your book.

When they request it, ask for their name, email, mailing address, and phone number. Ask them how interested they are in what you offer, and their time frame for the services or products that meet the need that you fill.

You now have what is called a LEAD - somebody who is interested in your information, and in your business.

This can also be done via a magazine ad, a newspaper ad, a radio ad, a billboard ad - or any other media. *HAVE a way and a reason for people to respond to your advertising.*

> *Pro Tip:* If you use advertising strategies to generate leads, I highly recommend having a tracking phone number. This is a phone number that automatically forwards calls to your office phone. At the end of each day/week/month, you get a report that says X calls came from ad #1, and Y calls came from ad #2. You can determine which ad pulls better, stop spending money on places/ads that don't work as well, and reallocate those marketing dollars to more of the ads that DO pull well.

TRANSFORMATION:

What way do you prefer people to contact you?

_____

_____

Strategy #7 - Incentivize Initial Appointments

If you are getting enough leads, but have difficulty getting appointments for visits or tours, use the book as a way to get that appointment. You could send them the book when they set an appointment, or you can give it to them when they actually show for the appointment. *This is EXTREMELY useful, and very underused.*

TRANSFORMATION:

Do people make appointments and not keep them? Yes/No

Use this space to create a short script to use within the conversation to GET them to keep their appointment. Here's a sample:

"Now Mary, when you get to the stable, I'll have a copy of my new book, (XYZ), waiting for you. It show you how to (get this result), and it's worth ($ value), but when you keep this appointment, it's yours at no charge."

_____

_____

_____

_____

_____

_____

Strategy #8 – Follow Up With Unconverted Prospects

If you generate leads and you get appointments, but not the sale, a book is a GREAT reason to follow up with those leads you already have now.

Using your book to convert a bank of unconverted leads can repay your investment for the entire program in a very short period of time. Call your leads and offer them the book as a thank you for coming in. Make sure it's autographed.

TRANSFORMATION:

Do people who should be buying from you visit, but not commit?

    Yes/No

Use this space to create a short script to use within the conversation to GET them to buy. Here's a sample:

"Now Mary, if you buy a block of 5 lessons, I'll have a copy of my new book, (XYZ), waiting for you. It show you how to (get this result), and it's worth ($ value), but when you buy the block of lessons, it's yours at no charge."

Strategy #9 – Give As A "Thank You" Gift

Use your book as a Thank You gift at ANY stage of your marketing process. Thank You for calling, Thank You for setting an appointment, Thank You for keeping your appointment, Thank You for visiting the facility, Thank You for signing up with us, Thank You for your business, Thank You for referring..

And of course you should autograph it, which makes it so much more special for the recipient!

TRANSFORMATION:

Things I can THANK my prospects/clients for:

1. _____
2. _____
3. _____
4. _____
5. _____
6. _____
7. _____
8. _____
9. _____
10. _____
11. _____

Strategy #10 – Capture Leads On Website

One thing I've noticed in my many years online is that many business owners are concerned with their ranking in the search engines. They want to be #1 for their keywords – which is natural. What's baffling that once I get to the website, I'm confused as to what they want me to do next.

What do you want people to DO on your site? Here's what I mean:

Let's say for a moment that I run a car dealership. Every day, people come into the business, they kinda look around, maybe they get into a car, they walk around a little bit, and then they leave.

It's madness to NOT send out a salesman. I want my salesmen talking to people who are looking at my cars – right?

Having a website that's well ranked is nearly completely useless unless you have a way to get a way to follow up with your visitors. That's why we get their name and email – so we can follow up with them over time, inviting them to become a customer.

And it's super easy when you have a book to offer a few chapters as an incentive to provide their contact info. In fact, if I met YOU at a networking event, a trade show, or if I sent you something in the mail, I invariably ask you for your email so I can send you follow up materials.

Let's go back to the car dealership example. I spent $1200 on advertising last week, and 12 people visit the store on Saturday. I've just paid $100 per visitor to bring them in. If I just let 11 of them walk out without buying anything, I have WASTED $1100. If only one person buys something, that means my "COST PER SALE" is $1200.

The list of things WRONG with that scenario is so long I could do a 2-day seminar on it. What could the car dealer owner do to cover his investment?

He could get each visitor's mailing and email address to send them coupons or sales announcements, or a bottle of leather cleaner or a pillow in the mail – it's not rocket science.

But so many business owners make this same exact mistake online. They spend tons of time, money, and energy to get people to their site – but then fail to get names and emails and phone numbers of interested prospects.

> So even if we DON'T end up working together, ask your webmaster about adding a lead capture system mechanism with a lead incentive and follow up system.. but don't be too surprised if he has no clue what any of that is, much less how to implement it

I'm passionate about this, and it pains me to no end to see honest business owners leaving so much money on the table, and/or wasting money when it really isn't necessary.

And it's unethical for people who sell advertising or media who can't or won't measure the results.

If we work together, not only do I do ALL this exciting and cool book stuff and media publicity for you, BUT we also measure the results that it brings in. You'll know the exact dollar amount it brings in.

There is no "spray and pray" marketing, no Hope Marketing here, where you cross your fingers and hope it works.

It's scientific, tracked, measured and proven. You see dollar-for-dollar your exact results when I handle any aspect of marketing for you.

TRANSFORMATION:

1. What my leads (prospects) are looking for (information leading to what result) when they visit my website: _____
2. If it were set up for me, I could gift them with a:
   - ☐ Chapter of my book
   - ☐ Checklist of some kind
   - ☐ Assessment or analysis of some kind
   - ☐ Other: _____

Strategy #11 - Send It As A Gift

If a client or a prospect doesn't already have your book, give it to them as a gift for a birthday, anniversary, a thank you, or as congratulations.

This is a great thing to do if you ever sponsor classes at shows or competitions, if you hold clinics at your facility, with other clinicians or you yourself: you can use the book to help drive registrations and/or attendance. If you want to use it to drive registrations, you send it out with their attendance information, after they have registered for the clinic. If you want it to drive attendance, to ensure people actually COME to the clinic, they get it when they check in.

Using it as a gift in a sponsored class is a little different. You might decide to hand it out to only those who place in the class, or you might choose to award it to everybody in the class. You'll want to make sure you bring enough to the show if you're going to give it to everybody in a class, and you may need help handing them out to class entrants, but it would make a HUGE impression on your target market to do it this way.

You want to be extremely selective about the class you sponsor, if you're going to hand them out to everybody, as you want to very carefully target your IDEAL client.

Either way, autographing it makes it ever so much more valuable to recipients. You can also use autographing a book as a means to build a bit of viral networking buzz – here's how.

Let's say I'm at a horse show or a trade event, like an expo, and Mary has just asked me for my autograph in a book I've just handed her. I've already gotten her business card if she has one. I'm always thrilled to autograph a book, so I intentionally DO NOT bring a pen to the conversation – I turn to John, who's standing nearby, in conversation with Susy, and I ask HIM for a pen.

Now John and Susy both want a book, and pretty soon a crowd gathers around, as I sign books, hand pens back (hopefully to the right owner) and borrow more, to sign a book for somebody else.

Just be sure to bring enough books! If you run out of books, get the name, phone #, mailing and email addresses of people who still want them.

TRANSFORMATION:

Ways I can GIFT my book:

1. Clients:
    a. Birthdays
    b. Great scores at a show...
    c. _____
2. Sponsor a class
    a. All entries
    b. Just Placers
3. Clinic attendees – upcoming clinics:
    a. _____
    b. _____
    c. _____
4. Expo or other type of horse trade show:
    a. _____
    b. _____
    c. _____
    d. _____
    e. _____

Strategy #12 – Build A Promotion

When your book is written correctly, it's a great tool for creating promotions. Giving away your book is easily tied to a holiday of your choice:

- ☐ New Year's
- ☐ Valentine's Day
- ☐ St. Patrick's Day
- ☐ April Fool's Day
- ☐ Memorial Day
- ☐ Father's Day
- ☐ Independence Day
- ☐ Back-To-School
- ☐ Labor Day
- ☐ Halloween
- ☐ Thanksgiving
- ☐ Christmas

Or any of many other holidays, recognition and awareness days. I can help you build any of these promotions ahead of time, so that it's ready to go.

TRANSFORMATION:

1. Check the box next to the holidays in the list above that you'd like to do a promo for.
2. Any others you'd like to add to the list?

    a. _____

    b. _____

    c. _____

    d. _____

    e. _____

    f. _____

    g. _____

    h. _____

Strategy #13 - Networking On Steroids

This is a strategy that I've actually already talked about. It's a high-powered strategy, one that resulted in a friend getting an offer for a position as an adjunct professorship – at the ripe old age of 23.

Go to the networking event. Don't bring business cards, just copies of your book. Walk around, chat with people, and hand them out. It's very high impact, very, very impressive.

Then offer to sign the book. If I'm talking with Mary, give her the book, then offer to sign it. DO NOT BRING A PEN – so that you can ask somebody else nearby, John, if he has a pen, so that I can autograph my book for Mary. Then he wants one, then an interested crowd gathers around you, and everybody wants a book.

Really cool, for everybody involved, really fun. This is a really memorable way to network. OF COURSE you get their card in exchange for the book, and you FOLLOW UP to get the appointment.

If you run out of books, KEEP ONE BOOK. Instead of handing them the book at this point, ask for their card, and offer to email something to them, like a special report (I can help with creating that). You can also mail a book or email a few chapters of the book too.

This strategy can be highly leveraged, so be careful with it! ;-)

TRANSFORMATION:

List of events you can use this strategy at:

1. Saddle club meeting
2. _____
3. _____

Strategy #14 - "Meet The Author"

S*tage and hold a "Meet the Author" event*, perhaps in conjunction with an open house, at your facility. You'll have a book signing where current and former clients and prospects come in for a free copy of your book, you sign it, and then you take a picture with them (their phone or yours). Post the pictures on your website, social media profiles, and you can have them share them as well.

You can even have the pictures printed up, framed, and given to them on the spot, or mailed a few days later.

This can also be further leveraged with strategies #1 (local media), #11 (Send it as a gift), & #15 (Create a Seminar).

Transformation:

Ideas for your "Meet the Author" event:

Where it will be held:_____

Who will be invited:

1. Clients
2. Public
3. Their friends - bonus if they bring a friend?

What else might take place?

1. Riding demos
2. Tack sale
3. Clinic
4. Other:

    _____

    _____

Strategy #15 – Create A Seminar

If you have the space to gather a number of people at one time, or if you can easily get one (it's super easy to get space at hotels, or even small local motels), invite your prospects to come and learn about what you do.

Offer a copy of your book for attending.

Also, be sure to record audio and video of your seminar event, which can be leveraged in the next strategy.

TRANSFORMATION:

Ideas for your seminar. Don't worry if you don't know all the pieces of this right now. I can assist you remotely.

1. Topic (same as your book – book is an outline of it): _____
2. Possible locations: _____
3. How to record:
    a. Audio _____
    b. Visuals _____
4. Who will make your PowerPoint: _____
5. Handouts/materials for participants: _____
    a. Handouts: _____
    b. Marketing materials: _____
    c. Who will make these: _____
6. How you'll market it: _____
7. Offer you'll make for participants: _____

Strategy #16 - Create Video or Audio Seminars

An audio seminar can be VERY easily put together, using a conference phone line. This is called a teleseminar. I personally have years of experience in putting these on - I've done over 100 of them, and can help you do one if we work together.

Rather than ask people to get in their vehicle and schlep to your facility or a hotel or library conference room, we invite them using my tested and proven process to simply call a phone number and listen to the presentation.

You are on the phone live, and present information on how your business is different and better, or it can be pre-recorded. At the end, you invite them to call your office, visit your website to set up an appointment, or whatever specific offer you chose.

An Audio + Visual online seminar is sometimes called a webinar, and it's sort of like a video seminar. It can be done live, or it can be recorded into a long video that we put on your website, on YouTube (or both). People are highly visual learners, and they retain more information from a video presentation when they watch and learn about you, your business, your book, what differentiates you, and what's in it for them.

Your book can be the basis on any presentation, so you don't have to prep much. Plus, if we work together, I can assist in putting things together for this sort of presentation.

Then, after the presentation has been recorded, it can be duplicated onto DVDs or CDs, which of course I also am skilled at, and can assist with. You can then send these in the mail to new prospects, bundle them with your book, etc.

You WANT to do this because:

1. The book establishes your status and authority.

2. Some people prefer to read material, others prefer to LISTEN to it, and still others prefer to WATCH.
3. Having all three, especially if you bundle them together, gives you a VERY unique marketing strategy – one that I can just about guarantee won't be duplicated by ANYBODY.

Why is this so important? Why go to all this work and effort and attention to detail?

BECAUSE – the biggest question people have in their minds, ESPECIALLY those who might have been affected by the recent recession – is this:

Who Can I TRUST?

If you educate, motivate, and qualify your target market by educating them, by providing VALUE, without being pushy, they appreciate it, and feel the need to reciprocate.

They want to get to know YOU, in a no- or low-pressure situation, so that they KNOW if they fit well with you, the way you teach, train, and interact with them and their horses.

They want to make a good decision, especially when it concerns their show career, and the well-being of their horse, so they want to go with the expert. Somebody who takes the time to educate them on HOW to properly MAKE the right decision is somebody they will work with.

*That's why *I* wrote this book that you are reading right now. That's why you are considering writing your own.*

We want people to listen to what we say before they run off and start talking to somebody else who doesn't know as much as we do about what we do best.

> ***Yes, this does apply in our industry.*** I'm available for consultation to see how it applies to your specific situation – please visit page 81 to learn how to get a FREE consultation with me.

TRANSFORMATION:

Ideas for your teleseminar. Don't worry if you don't know all the pieces of this right now. I can assist you remotely.

1. Topic (same as your book – book is an outline of it): _____
2. Handouts/materials for participants: _____
    a. Handouts: _____
    b. Marketing materials: _____
    c. Who will make these: _____
3. How you'll market it: _____
4. Offer you'll make for participants: _____
5. What you might do with the recording: _____

Ideas for your webinar:

1. Topic (same as your book – book is an outline of it): _____
2. Handouts/materials for participants: _____
    a. Handouts: _____
    b. Marketing materials: _____
    c. Who will make these: _____
3. How you'll market it: _____
4. Offer you'll make for participants: _____
5. What you might do with the recording: _____

Strategy #17 - Online Marketing

Just as we just took your book and turned it into an live seminar, an audio teleseminar, a webinar, put them online and on CDs and DVDs, your book content can very easily be used to create marketing content online for social media and search engine rankings.

Here are just a few of the many, many ways we can use your book online:

- Snippets of content posted on Facebook, Twitter, LinkedIn, SEO+, and other social media profiles. Can be text, images, or short videos.
- Posting a piece of a chapter on your blog helps improve SEO, and the resulting improvement increases organic traffic to your site.
- Posting pieces of chapters of different blog sites such as WordPress.com, Blogspot, Tumbler, and many others.
- Create short videos or audio recordings and post them on video sites and podcast directories. You can easily have a series of videos on YouTube, Vimeo, Metacafe, and Daily Motion, all of which improve your search engine positions. Audio recordings can be posted on podcasts like iTunes and others.
- If you combine the book with strategies #1 and #2, you can announce your media presence on your social media profiles and your website, greatly compounding the effects of credibility and new traffic to your website, your book, and your business.

TRANSFORMATION:

1. Does this sound like a good idea?
    a. Yes
    b. No
2. Can I do it myself, or do I need help implementing it?
    a. DIY
    b. Need assistance
    c. Don't know...

I'*ve handed you 17 great strategies for leveraging your new book.* These are brilliant, highly leveraged marketing ideas that will generate new clients for you.

You don't have to use ALL of them, just using a few will more than pay for your writing and marketing packages.

But far-and-away, the single best strategy to using a book is to use it to get referrals... tons of referrals...

Strategy #18 - How To Use Your Book To Generate Referrals

Of course you already know what a referral is. Mary boards her horse at your facility, her friend Sarah is looking for a place, or is dissatisfied with where she is, or visits Mary and likes your facility, so arranges to move her horse there.

Referrals are the least costly way to get the best clients. It is also one of the least understood marketing strategies, and therefore one of the most underutilized ones.

So how do you leverage your new book to get your referral program hopping?

One of the best ways is to use it to create Offline Viral Marketing. You've heard of viral marketing - it's when Mary sees your video, shares it on her Facebook profile, then 10 of her friends see and love and share it, then 100 of theirs, and so on. It's a compounding, exponential exposure for your business.

In real life, it usually compounds only so far, then dies out. Some businesses live and die by it. For most, it's a lot of work, and it doesn't go as far as the model might indicate.

It can however, be somewhat replicated OFFLINE. You can indeed use the concept of viral marketing and word-of-mouth, and one of the easiest, best ways to start, is to give your book away to people who are "Centers of Influence." These are people who know and who are respected, by groups of people who are likely to use your facility's services.

This is called the "Offline Viral Marketing" strategy. Here's how it works:

1. *Identify a person* (or group) who has friends, family, coworkers, peers, members, customers, clients, patients or network connections that you wish to serve.
2. *Give this person a number of copies of your book.* The number you give them depends on the size of their network. For example, if you wanted

to reach a person's family members, you might give them 2 or 3 books. If they are a tack shop or feed store, you might leave a dozen or even a box of books, depending on the activity in the store, and their connection to the market.
3. *That center of influence gives away your books* to their family members or customers or members.
4. *THOSE people, in turn, connect with you* by phone or website or however you've chosen, so they can take the next step in becoming a client.

So first off, who can you GIVE those books to, so that they can pass them on to your target audience on your behalf?

- *Start with your current clients.* Give each current client at least 2-3 books, and specifically ask them to share them. "Here you are, Mary. I want you to have a copy of my new book. I also want you to have a few to share with friends or family that might also be interested in learning more. How many do you realistically think you need – how many friends do you have that are interested in dressage (or whatever your specialty is)?"
- *Tack and feed stores that service your geographic market area.* Make a list of relevant ones. If your specialty is dressage, for example, you *might* not want to include a tack shop that sells ONLY western goods – as an example. That's a judgment call. Or you could test it, as when people call you, you should ask WHERE they got their book. Then you'll know which places to keep stocked in the future.

After making your list, call each, explaining that you're a new local equine author, and would they be willing to give a book to each customer – would their customers be interested in that. If you present it right, they might even be willing to do an email blast to their customer list, and invite them to come in and get a book for free (or even free with purchase)!

- *Local Horse Clubs, Groups, Associations, Societies*, etc, as relevant. Sometimes these are willing to work directly with you, just as I've described the tack and feed shops. Other times, they might be happier if you came and did a presentation, then offered your book for free to attendees. Groups that meet on a regular basis are often looking for presenters. Others, especially larger ones, realize they need to monetize their connection power, so they ask us to become a sponsor (pay them for the privilege).
- *Leverage the book to get speaking engagements.* As I mentioned above, many groups look for speakers. As you give your presentation, make references back to your book. At the end of the presentation, invite people to the back of the room, or to your booth, or where ever you've stashed your books, to come up and get an autographed copy. Get business cards from the "centers of influence" that you meet there, and leverage them to move up to bigger and bigger opportunities.

This Offline Viral Marketing strategy can be combined with all the other strategies we've discussed.

And, it's so effective because it combines expert status, authority positioning, and celebrity with an IMPLIED ENDORSEMENT of the tack shop, the local association, or whatever/whomever your center of influence is, which is very similar to what you get with referrals. It's really like taking a referral "fire" and dumping gallons of gasoline on it.

Transformation 13: REFERRALS STRATEGY

1. Can you give your book to your current clients to generate referrals?
    a. YES _____
    b. NO_____
    c. MAYBE_____

2. Would they take them?
    a. YES _____
    b. NO_____

c. MAYBE_____

3. Would they pass them on to friends, family, coworkers, peers, etc.?
   a. YES _____
   b. NO_____
   c. MAYBE_____

4. Are you a member of any networking groups (think horse associations, societies, clubs, etc), where you could donate your books, and/or offer an educational presentation or class on your service?
   a. _____
   b. _____
   c. _____
   d. _____

5. Do you know of any businesses n your area that COULD refer to you but aren't currently? Where else serves the people you wish to reach?
   a. _____
   b. _____
   c. _____
   d. _____

6. Do you think that if you used your book, that you might get some of them to refer to you (give away your book, either for free, or as a gift-with-purchase)?
   a. YES _____
   b. NO_____
   c. MAYBE_____

7. Are there any centers of influence you'd LIKE to reach, but haven't been able to connect with?

a. _____
b. _____
c. _____
d. _____

8. Do you think that if you sent a FedEx package with your book, some testimonials, your CD or DVD, and a brief introductory letter that you might get some of them on the phone?
    a. YES _____
    b. NO_____
    c. MAYBE_____

Chapter

14

Frequently Asked Questions

Direct Response Marketing vs. "Hope" Marketing – How do I know what I'm using?

If you don't know, you're probably using "Hope Marketing." Direct Response Marketing entails a bit of education to implement, or, if you have somebody else setting up technical things for you, to understand the strategies and tactics. Understanding these things is more important than having the technical know-how to set them up. Tech can be hired. YOU NEED to understand WHY you are doing what you are doing.

The easy way to determine is to decide if your marketing efforts are more focused on:

- Branding yourself in the market, or on
- Getting a specific RESPONSE from the market, learning specifically WHICH marketing pulls and which does not, and using what works once you know.

It's your ship, your destiny. YOU need to be in control of it.

Why do "I" (or my business) need a book?

We use the properly-written book as an under-the-radar marketing piece to achieve these objectives:

1. Get your facility (or yourself) the publicity you WANT, but which you cannot get on your own.

2. Get the attention of your IDEAL client, and get them into your sales process. We set up the conversation so that they are chasing YOU, rather than you chasing THEM.
3. Indoctrinate new or current IDEAL clients, so they are fully aware of the full extent of your offering, and so they don't go over to a competitor.
4. You are established as the preeminent authority in your niche – the standard all others are judged by.

WHAT IS THE RIGHT WAY TO SET UP MY BOOK?

The RIGHT way to set up the book is to have somebody else do it. This is a sophisticated marketing piece, not a literary work or a biography or fiction – although a great many of THOSE are also "ghost written."

You need to focus on running your business – on giving riding lessons, training horses, competing horses for clients, keeping your stallion happy – whatever it is that you do best.

You DON'T want to do ALL the work of writing the book, and setting up the website – only to find out after investing hours of your precious time that you did it wrong, negating all the valuable time you spent working on the project and wasting both your time and money.

WHAT IS THE "RIGHT WAY" TO SET UP MY WEBSITE?

The RIGHT WAY to set up your website is to set it up as a forced-optin, direct response marketing machine, with an automatic followup email sequence. It forces people to get on your email list in order to see more. It automatically follows up with them to get them to take the actions you specify.

You MUST be selective here, to ask people to jump through hoops, because your book is sending highly qualified individuals to you; you WANT them to disqualify themselves, AND you have an "ethical bribe" behind that optin gate.

If people are visiting the site in order to GET your book, we'll have an option for them as well.

How Can a Book "Fence IN" My Herd (clients)?

Here are three ways in which your book will protect your clients from poaching by a competitor:

- **First, it programs current clients** to look at your competition in a new light, from a new perspective... the perspective YOU want them to use. Reading is a wonderful way to program (or reprogram) our minds, or those of our clients. You can literally program your IDEAL Client to STAY at your facility. It's a great way to reinforce the fences you have around your herd.
- **Second, you can easily use it to get prospects to qualify** or disqualify themselves, making your job much easier. The more IDEAL clients you have, the fewer total clients you even need.
- **Third, use your book to indoctrinate new clients**, to ensure they are getting the most out of working with you, that you have less corrective work to do to get them on track, on board, and running smoothly in their new "horse home."

In short, it protects your business, automates your customer retention and lead-generation work, and is a great "client orientation" tool, leading to greater customer retention.

How do I get word out about my new book?

In the last chapter, I gave you 18 different strategies to use to get your book out. Pick one and go with it. Then leverage it with some others.

Depending on the package you decide on, I can help you connect with your regular clients and even new clients via email, postal mail, and social media.

We'll work together with your local media, bookstores, feed and tackshops to set up interviews with media, books and signing events in those places, as well as possibly set up an event at your facility.

You'll want to hand them out (or sell them) at events like expos, horse shows, and the like, using it like a business card. Use the strategies I gave you in the last chapter to ramp up how well that works for you.

We can also set up your site so people can order your new book from it, and connect with you after they've read the book.

You can – and SHOULD – use it to magnify and amp up your current marketing. Your book is a GREAT leverage point to use with your current marketing strategies.

WHY SHOULD I LET YOU DO IT FOR ME INSTEAD OF A GHOSTWRITER I KNOW?

Because your ghostwriter friend might be a good writer.. but they aren't good at direct response marketing. Or, more likely, even marketing at all. They are just writers. That is all they do. Beyond crafting a highly specialized marketing piece, we are crafting a highly specialized marketing strategy – not just an instructional book. You need somebody who knows what to write to get your reader to take the actions you desire, and then to further funnel and move them along your sales path.

Because I do it the right way, the first time. There is sooo much going on under the hood of this thing, that even I only trust people I PERSONALLY KNOW are expert Direct Response Marketers to even consider thinking about doing this on their own.. and even then, 90% of them will get a lot of it wrong.

Because YOU need to focus on running your business, not on building new marketing pieces for it. And certainly nothing as complicated as this machine is to get all up and running.

Because I'm experienced at this . I've been around the block, I've been there, done that. And for the technical pieces I'm not so personally good at, I have a crack team ready to jump in and do their amazing stuff. Rule #1 is always "Do What You Do BEST." That's why you have a farrier, a vet, a massage therapist, a groom, an auto repair guy and your personal hair stylist in your rolodex. Better they do those things than you in most cases.

Because I am an equestrian myself. I know as horsepeople we have our own language that we use – we use terms within our industry that mean something specific only to us. We know merely by how those terms are used if somebody is savvy or not to our horse language, and therefore, how much of an expert they are. I also know that within each discipline and sport we have terms that are even more specific. I am sensitive to that, and your terminology needs to be reflected in your book.

Because I WILL get you on local media-at the very least.

I know how to get you into the local media – TV/Radio stations, newspapers, regional horse magazines and so forth. If your business and your book call for it, I get you national media too.

This is not a "spray-and-pray" approach, either. You're prepped and ready to go with my organized approach. All the pieces are in place, and you'll look and sound great.

Because of the power of this, it's only offered as part of the advanced marketing package.

Because I offer a 8-Way, 100% Money-back, satisfaction guarantee – Remember, you get what you pay for. I personally guarantee that you'll:

1. NOT have to write the book yourself.
2. Get your rough draft within 7-10 days of our interview
3. Have final say over what is published.

4. Approve of the cover, and that I'll have several options for you within just a few days of our interview.
5. Have books in your hands, provided you get feedback to me in a timely manner, within 4-6 weeks of our initial interview.
6. Be so amazed at the results you see in your business stemming from publishing your book that you'll happily leave me a glowing endorsement.
7. Exclusivity within a pre-determined radius (typically 50 miles of your zip code), by discipline.
8. ROI that makes you happy that you invested.

Try finding **any** ghostwriter or marketing specialist who offers ANY kind of guarantee - they are few and far between.

WHAT IS YOUR PROCESS?

Once I've given you the green light and accepted you as a client, we schedule an interview by phone.

1. I'll outline the milestones and when payments are due.
2. We'll go through your answers to the Transformation exercises in this book, (plus a few more), so I understand your business and your objectives completely.
3. Then we set up the structure of the book, and I ask questions as we go, which is the content.
4. We can spend up to 4 hours total interviewing - these may be 30-minute, 60-minute or up to 2-hour blocks of time.
5. I'll write a rough draft of the book, and send it to you for approval. You'll also get sample covers to approve.
6. I finish up the manuscript, get it printed, and send you a supply of books.

When you opt for a premium package, we determine exactly what you require, and then set up that marketing.

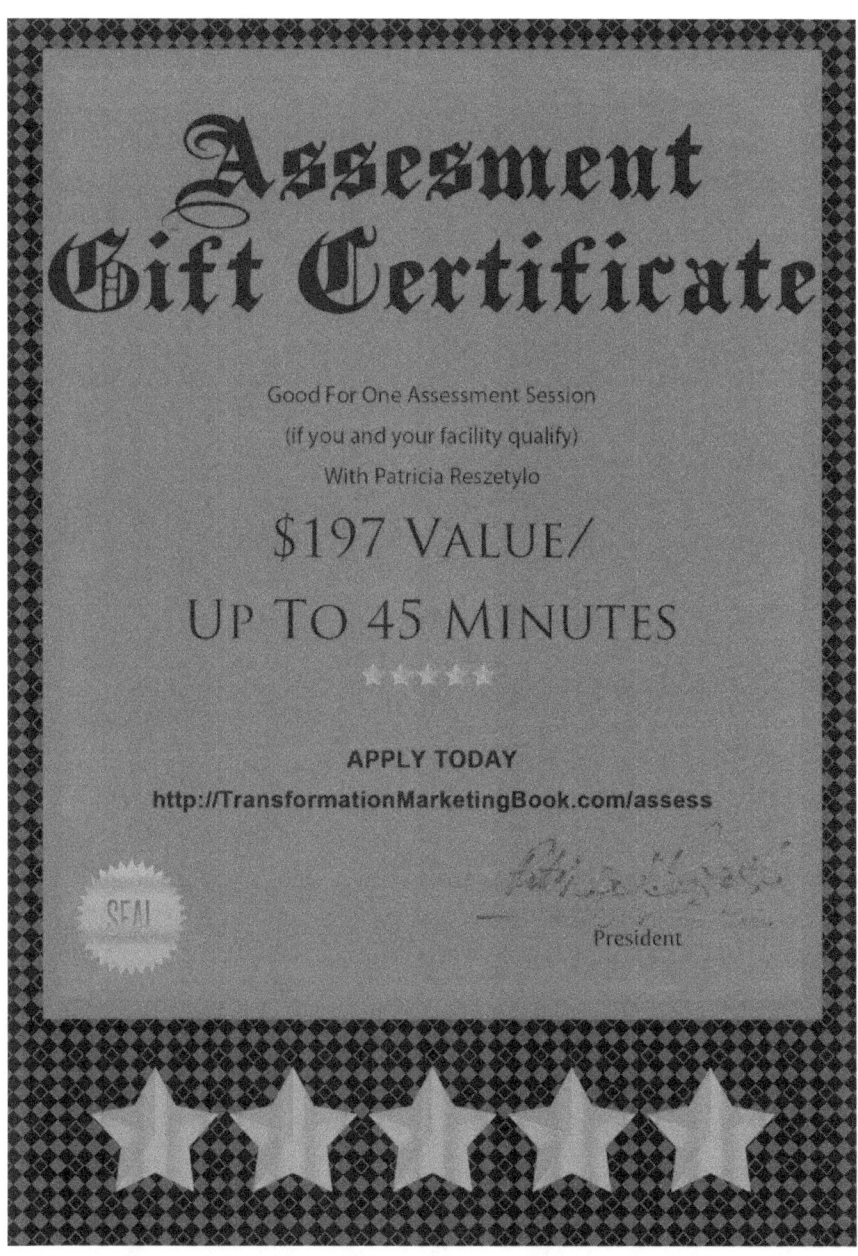

NEXT STEP:

First, I suggest thinking about a book title for your book. Here are a few suggestions to get you started – just tick the ones you think are interesting:

- ☐ What To Know About Choosing The Best Dressage Facility In The Dallas Area
- ☐ What To Know About Choosing The Best (your specialty) Facility in The (your area)
- ☐ (_____) That Other (_____) Don't Want You To Know About
- ☐ How To Confidently Choose The Best (_____)
- ☐ How To (get this great benefit)
- ☐ Top (number) Of Ways To (get a benefit your service provides)
- ☐ (Number of) Things Your Current (_____) Won't Tell You
- ☐ How To (do something) (fast, easy, cheap)
- ☐ How To (deal with a common problem)
- ☐ How (your solution) (provides an awesome benefit)
- ☐ Using (your solution) To (provide specific benefit)
- ☐ The (target audience)'s Guide To (what you do)

Think about the benefits your product or service provides, and the problems you solve for your clients. Then make it fast, easy, simple.

Remember, your book is to establish your authority, credibility, and expertise. It must properly educate your target audience with the things they need to know before they can make a decision, and it must motivate them to work with you. What questions do you WANT people to ask? What questions do your IDEAL clients ask?

It's also a device we can use to bring up and handle the objections people often bring up during the sales process. This will help you streamline closing sales, saving you time and making you money.

Then, to apply for your assessment, please visit the website at http://TransformationMarketingBook.com/consult, where you'll:

- Learn more about the process
- **Fill out and submit** the assessment application.
- **Give me a few days** to go over your application and see if we fit.
- **If we ARE a fit,** we'll set up an appointment for your phone assessment, and you'll get your homework assignment.

If we are NOT a fit, I'll let you know. I'll not waste your valuable time.

Conclusion

Navigating the marketing for your facility, services, product or sponsorship opportunity is tricky, even though the recession has passed. Your IDEAL clients ARE out there – but you have to PROVE your value to them.

You need a marketing strategy that:

- *Sets you apart from the herd*,
- *Positions* you as an authority in your niche,
- *Presents you as the only logical option* for your market, and
- *Doesn't interfere with your daily duties* or distract you from what you do best.

The properly written book, coupled with proper direct response marketing and website does that heavy lifting for you.

Are you ready to take your facility's marketing up a significant notch? Are you ready to make a REAL splash in the marketplace? Ready to stop competing with other facilities in your area, and REALLY establish yours as the ONE-AND-ONLY place to go for your sport/discipline?

If you're ready to move ahead, then take the NEXT STEP – connect with me and get started building your future.

I look forward to hearing from you, learning more about your business, and how I can best serve you!

Patricia Reszetylo,
Author of Transformation Marketing For Upscale Equine Facilities

GLOSSARY
Clients:

- IDEAL – Your best clients, who pay you the most to do the work you enjoy the most. They have the best profit margins, are the most enjoyable to be around and work with. These are the ones you want to clone'
- DUD – Your WORST clients. They are slow to pay, pick and choose services ala cart rather than through packages, are the least pleasant to be with, have the thinnest profit margins. These are the ones you'd LIKE to get rid of.
- AVERAGE – This is when you take all your clients, and lump them into one single group, instead of segmenting them into IDEAL and DUD. Yes, you should know what your average client is like. It's more important to know your IDEAL and look for more of them.

Direct Response Marketing (DRM) – Marketing that asks the target market to respond in a single specific manner. That might entail visiting a website and opting in to your email list, it might be picking up the phone and calling a pre-recorded message, or it might be to do something else. It has evolved from mail-order marketing, and now can be used in any kind of business.. including yours.

Direct Marketing – See Direct Response Marketing.

Equestrian – Typically construed as a person who rides a horse, but also includes others who work with them. A person who competes with a horse in halter or driving is in fact an equestrian.

Facility – A horse business with stables. It might include riding or driving arenas, race tracks, jumping courses, dressage maneges, and so forth.

Hope Marketing – The process of "doing marketing things" that the business owner HOPES are working, but without any real strategic direction, and without any tracking to know IF a strategy or tactic is working (or how well it is working).

All marketing must be tracked to know if/how well it works, as well as how good the clients that come in through it perform for the company.

Marketing – Any and all activities that work together to position and bring in revenues for the business. This not only includes advertising, but also includes things seemingly unrelated such as WHERE one advertises, the clients one accepts, how the facility is kept up, perhaps even the vehicle that is driven by the owner. Customer service is a big part of marketing strategy for many businesses.

Pareto Principle – (also known as the **80-20 rule**, the **law of the vital few**, and the **principle of factor sparsity**) states that, for many events, roughly 80% of the effects come from 20% of the causes. **Management consultant Joseph M. Juran** suggested the principle and named it after Italian **economist Vilfredo Pareto**, who observed in 1906 that 80% of the land in Italy was owned by 20% of the population; Pareto developed the principle by observing that 20% of the pea pods in his garden contained 80% of the peas.

It is a common **rule of thumb** in business; e.g., "80% of your sales come from 20% of your clients". Mathematically, the 80-20 rule is roughly followed by a **power law** distribution (also known as a **Pareto distribution**) for a particular set of parameters, and many natural phenomena have been shown empirically to exhibit such a distribution. [4]

Upscale - relating to the more expensive or affluent sector of the market. An upscale client will spend more on their hobbies/passions because they CAN, and are more insulated from economic flux than a middle class client. <u>An upscale facility understands</u> and caters to this market, can offer better

---

[4] http://en.wikipedia.org/wiki/Pareto_principle

service and better experiences than a run of the mill one that has all middle-class clientele.

---

[i] Did you figure it out? The pink, clapping bunny, aka, The Energizer Bunny, sells Energizer Batteries. I know, I usually forget it too!

www.ingramcontent.com/pod-product-compliance
Lightning Source LLC
Chambersburg PA
CBHW071723170526
45165CB00005B/2124